TALES OF
THE PEA SEA

BY ROBERT McEWEN

DRAMA

Human Resources
Cholo!
Negative Image
The Pull Toy
Son Of A Gonne

FICTION

Raymond And Regina
Transition Game

NON-FICTION

Journey: 75 Years Of Kodak Research

TALES OF
THE PEA SEA

◆

Playlets, Poems & Potpourri

by
Robert McEwen

To Wendy and Larry,
In friendship and
appreciation.
Warm regards,
Bob

iUniverse, Inc.
New York Lincoln Shanghai

TALES OF THE PEA SEA
Playlets, Poems & Potpourri

iUniverse, Inc.

For information address:
iUniverse, Inc.
2021 Pine Lake Road, Suite 100
Lincoln, NE 68512
www.iuniverse.com

ISBN: 0-595-31918-1

Printed in the United States of America

To Karen and Kenny

Satire's my weapon, but I'm too discreet
To run amuck, and tilt at all I meet.

Alexander Pope

Contents

Author's Notes And Acknowledgements

The works in this anthology were written during my fellowship in the Iowa Playwrights Workshop from 1992 through 1995. The satires in particular are informed by the polarizing events of that period, including the travails of the Clinton Administration, the presidential candidacy of Pat Buchanan, the aftermath of the Clarence Thomas-Anita Hill hearings, and the abortion debates that rose to fever pitch in those years.

Mostly, however, the works are informed by own emotional response to artistic and intellectual life on the University of Iowa campus. I found myself suddenly buffeted by powerful and relentless currents in that sea of political orthodoxy, and sought to swim against those currents while maintaining a sense of humor and the friendships of those with whom I disagreed on almost every public policy issue.

Ten years after these pieces were written, it remains an inscrutable mystery to me why the institution encouraged every conceivable kind of diversity—except diversity of political opinion. On that score, a prescribed line of thinking was not only encouraged but often enforced—in ways that sometimes were subtle and sometimes were not.

My response simply was to sheath alternative points of view in the voices of my characters, leaving the cultural thought police apoplectic over my work but impotent to attack it without placing themselves in opposition to artistic freedom.

While the Left certainly takes its lumps in these playlets, so, too, do Big Business and, in one poem, the Catholic Church. Indeed, whereas my former fellow artists in the Iowa workshop are pleasantly surprised by my opposition to the present Bush Administration's unfortunate adventurism in Iraq, they smile knowingly in recognition of my seemingly inextinguishable anger over the self-aggrandizing behavior of bureaucrats who abuse authority in academia, business, government, religion, and the media.

For helping me survive Iowa without sacrificing my artistic integrity, I would like to thank the following writers, actors, directors, designers, mentors, and friends: Jannette Bailey, Shelley Berc, Shelby Brammer, Kent Braverman, Lad Brown, Lyle Browne, Edie Campbell, Sandy Cavanaugh, Katie Censky, Maggie Conroy, Paul Donnelly, Eric Ehn, Michael Grecco, Dave Guerdette, Keith Huff, Van Jenkins, Ne' Le'au, Byungha and Yong-Ju Lim, Jack Lynch, Don McClure, Cassandra Medley, John Morning, Lavonne Mueller, John O'Keefe, Dene Oneida, Lanie Robertson, Pat Robertson, Howard Stein, Peter Sukovaty, Nabe Yaya Swaray, Sergei Task, Janelle and Jennifer Vanerstrom, Frank and Teresa Wagner, Tom Waites and Tim Wisgerhof.

Tales Of
The Pea Sea

Once upon a time, many years ago, in a land far away, an old Mariner sailed his ship toward a harbor where there lived a community of fishermen and their families. The ship's hull held a cargo of fruits and vegetables for the fishermen, who had endured a long winter and were desperately in need of the food.

Access to the harbor was controlled by the operator of a drawbridge, a Sea Hag, who raised and lowered its grating to allow passage. No one had elected or appointed her to the post. She merely usurped it one day, and no one challenged her for fear she would accuse them publicly of being insensitive to sea hags.

When the Mariner approached the harbor and called upon the Sea Hag to raise the bridge, she refused, exclaiming, "You can't come in here with that ship!"

The Mariner asked, innocently enough, "Why not?"

The Sea Hag responded, "Why not? Just look at that figurehead on your bow!"

The Mariner looked at the figurehead. It was a beautifully-carved, hand-painted figure of the head and torso of a fisherman.

The Mariner said, "I don't understand. What's the problem?"

The Sea Hag, apoplectic at his failure to understand, screamed at the Mariner: "You can't sail that ship into this harbor! You'll offend the fishermen!"

The Mariner, astonished by her vehemence, asked, "Why will they be offended?"

The Sea Hag, now spitting mad, said, "Just look at that figure! He's got a salt-and-pepper beard, leathery skin, wizened eyes, he's wearing a turned-up, lemon-yellow rain hat and slicker, and he's smoking a corn-cob pipe!"

The Mariner said, "So?"

And the Sea Hag shot back, "You're perpetuating a stereotype! The fishermen won't stand for it!"

The Mariner replied, "But I've got five fishermen on the crew of this ship. None of <u>them</u> are offended by that statue."

The Sea Hag said, "Well, they <u>ought</u> to be. Maybe they need the money, and <u>have</u> to work on your ship, and can't help being exploited. Or maybe they're just ignorant, and don't know any better. Perhaps this incident will raise their consciousness."

The Mariner replied, "That's ridiculous. It was a fisherman who carved that piece of wood, and another fisherman who painted it, and another fisherman who mounted it on the bow of my ship."

The Sea Hag dismissed this argument. "Those facts are irrelevant," she said. "I know these people. I know the fishermen of this community. And I know they will be offended."

"But <u>you're</u> not a fisherman," the Mariner said. "Why don't you let them decide for themselves what offends them?"

"Very well" said the Sea Hag, who retreated momentarily to her small guardhouse, then returned, accompanied this time by a fisherman who the Mariner recognized as Benedict, a former member of his crew.

"Look at that figurehead, Benedict," the Sea Hag said. "Is it, or is it not offensive to fishermen?"

Benedict hung his head and pawed at the ground with his foot, then said, "It is."

The Sea Hag pressed him further: "It is <u>what</u>, Benedict?"

"It is offensive."

"And <u>why</u> is it offensive, Benedict?"

"Because it perpetuates stereotypes of fishermen," he said, reciting the words in a familiar, singsong fashion.

"Very good, Benedict," the Sea Hag said, handing Benedict a cookie. She then turned to the Mariner and said, "See. I told you the fishermen would be offended."

"But Benedict," the flabbergasted Mariner said to his former shipmate. "You were with us when the statue was carved, and you expressed admiration for the woodwork. You were with us when the statue was painted, and you complimented the artist. You even helped to hoist the statue when we affixed it to the bow. If you found it so offensive, why didn't you say something then?"

"I don't know," Benedict said. "I guess I wasn't offended then."

"Well," the Mariner asked, "When <u>did</u> you become offended?"

"I don't know. I guess it was after the Sea Hag told me it was offensive."

The Sea Hag smiled a crooked smile and handed Benedict another cookie as the Mariner gaped incredulously at the two of them.

"Well, what are you waiting for?" the Sea Hag said to the Mariner. "Turn your ship around and sail off to some <u>un</u>enlightened port."

So the Mariner turned his ship about and sailed away. The fruits and vegetables rotted in the hull of his ship, and three children of the village died of scurvy that spring. Their parents grieved terribly, until the Sea Hag came to visit and explained to them that, although the death of children is a sad thing, their sacrifice had not been in vain because a greater good was achieved: no subculture had been offended.

THE END

Minnesota Twins

CAST OF CHARACTERS

Identical twins Edwina and Wilma Withers
A handful of sportswriters
A very tall man
A bald friar

SETTING

A news conference

TIME

1994

AT RISE:

Identical twin sisters approach a podium for a press conference. They are dead serious. Not a trace of humor in their appearances, their facial expressions, or—when they speak—their voices.

EDWINA

Good morning. My name is Edwina Withers.

WILMA

And I am Wilma Withers.

EDWINA

Thank you for coming. It is gratifying to see that so many members of both the local and national media have turned out today for what we believe is a very important announcement.

WILMA

This morning, on behalf of the estimated one million, seven hundred forty thousand pairs of twins in the United States, we call upon the management of the Minnesota Twins Baseball Team of the American League and Major League Baseball, Incorporated, to henceforth cease and desist from use of the nickname "Twins."

EDWINA

We find it highly offensive that this term is employed as a nickname for a major league sports franchise.

WILMA

We call upon the management of the Minnesota team to remove the word "Twins" from all uniforms, caps, gloves, t-shirts, bats, programs, pennants, and souvenirs, and from all other promotional materials designed for either print or broadcast use.

EDWINA

Our reasons should be clear to everyone. We find it abominable that in 1994, a purportedly responsible business enterprise would continue to perpetuate a demeaning stereotype.

WILMA

Twins, like other emergent minority groups, will no longer tolerate such insidious characterizations.

EDWINA

Like race, gender, or sexual orientation, being born a twin is not something over which one has any choice.

WILMA

We cannot change, nor would we want to.

EDWINA

You can imagine the outcry over a team named the New York Negroes.

WILMA

Or the New Jersey Jews.

EDWINA

The Chicago Chinamen.

WILMA

The Forth Worth Wetbacks.

EDWINA

The Houston Homosexuals.

WILMA

The Baltimore Broads.

EDWINA

The Los Angeles Lesbians.

WILMA

The Dallas Dykes.

EDWINA

The Gulf Coast Geezers.

WILMA

The Kansas City Cripples.

EDWINA

The Boston Blind.

WILMA

The Richmond Retarded.

EDWINA

Or the Denver Deaf.

WILMA

We find the designation "Minnesota Twins" equally offensive.

EDWINA

We do not appreciate being portrayed as mascots alongside animals such as the Detroit Tigers and the Chicago Cubs.

WILMA

Twins are people, not beasts.

EDWINA

And we've decided to resist a longstanding appellation that has had the effect of dehumanizing us.

WILMA

Beginning with tomorrow's season opener, we are calling for twins everywhere...

EDWINA

...and their families, friends, and acquaintances...

WILMA

...to join us in a nationwide boycott of all Twins games, both home and away.

EDWINA

Moreover, we call upon minority employees of the Minnesota Twins organization...

WILMA

...African-Americans...

EDWINA

...Asian-Americans...

WILMA

...Hispanic-Americans...

EDWINA

...Native Americans...

WILMA

...Women...

EDWINA

...Gays...

WILMA

...Lesbians...

EDWINA

…Senior citizens…

WILMA

…the visually impaired…

EDWINA

…the hearing-impaired…

WILMA

…and the physically-challenged…

EDWINA

…to show solidarity and join us in this action by walking off their jobs until such time as the Minnesota management meets our demands.

WILMA

In addition, we appeal to the chambers of commerce of both Minneapolis and St. Paul to cease and desist use of the term "Twin Cities."

EDWINA

We are not bricks and concrete and skyscrapers.

WILMA

We are flesh and blood, just like any other group of people.

EDWINA

All we ask is the same measure of respect that is accorded to other human beings.

Pause. The TWINS turn and nod at each other.

WILMA

At this point, we are ready to field questions.

EDWINA *(gesturing)*

Yes, the reporter from the Star & Tribune.

STAR & TRIBUNE

I'm afraid I just can't buy the comparisons you're making with other minority groups. The situation just isn't the same.

EDWINA and WILMA look at each other. When WILMA speaks, her tone is ominous, as if she is issuing a warning.

WILMA

I think you ought to be **very** careful in your use of the word "same."

Long pause.

EDWINA

In many contexts, it can be very offensive to twins.

WILMA

Words such as "identical" or "similar" or "replica" also are fraught with subliminal meanings.

EDWINA

Phrases such as "same old, same old"...

WILMA

...and "spitting image"...

EDWINA

...and "dead ringer"...

WILMA

...are often used as code words by those seeking to advance a hidden political agenda that works against the interests of twins.

EDWINA

A word such as "unique"—when used in the presence of twins, but referring to a non-twin—subtly denigrates those of us who share certain physical characteristics with others.

WILMA

And phrases such as "individual initiative," for example, can imply that twins are lazy.

EDWINA

So, you can see why eliminating offensive speech from the general lexicon is among our foremost objectives.

WILMA

We regard it as one of our most urgent national priorities.

EDWINA *(gesturing)*

Yes, the reporter from the *Post-Dispatch*.

POST-DISPATCH

What <u>in</u>offensive term would you substitute for words such as "same" or "similar"?

The TWINS confer for a moment.

WILMA

We prefer the term…

EDWINA and **WILMA** *(together, in unison)*

…"differentially challenged"…

The compliant reporter nods and dutifully scribbles down the term in his notepad. All of the gathered media readily accept the wisdom of this change in journalistic vocabulary. The TWINS scan the room as if to invite additional questions, but see no raised hands.

EDWINA

If there are no more questions at this point, we would like to proceed by introducing two special guests…

*A **VERY TALL MAN** and a **BALD MONK** wearing a brown robe and sandals join the TWINS at the podium.*

WILMA

They will address their remarks to the owners of the San Francisco Giants and the San Diego Padres.

EDWINA

Gentlemen?

END OF PLAY

The Cheerleaders Split

CAST OF CHARACTERS

Becky: late 20s, liberal
Megan: late 20s, conservative
Nigel: early 30s, English upper crust
Sal: early 30s, Italian working class
Waitress: 40s, country-western

SETTING

A truck stop café on Interstate 80 midway between Denver and Chicago.

TIME

The early 1990s.

FADE IN:

INT.   TRUCKSTOP   DAY

Two couples in their late twenties enter from opposite ends and head toward the same vacant booth.

MEGAN
Becky?

BECKY
Megan?

They embrace and jump up and down, re-enacting a high school cheer as their spouses smile politely at one another.

MEGAN & BECKY
R-A-M-S! (faster) R-A-M-S! The best!

Their spouses shake hands and nod at each other's wives.

NIGEL
Nigel St. John-Smythe.

SAL
Sal Santangelo.

The women are already in the booth reminiscing. Their husbands slide in beside their wives.

BECKY
I can't believe this!

MEGAN
What's it been? Ten years?

BECKY
Where are you coming from? Where are you going?

MEGAN
We're going to Denver. There's a—

BECKY
We live in Denver!

MEGAN
Oh, if only we'd known!

BECKY
Of all weekends. Denver is a madhouse. There's going to be one of those awful right-to-life rallies with pickled fetuses and—

BECKY's POV: CLOSE UP *of a campaign button on Megan's lapel reading "Abortion Stops A Beating Heart."*

TRACK UP *slowly to Megan's face. She is crestfallen.*

SAL breaks the uncomfortable silence.

SAL
Uh, where are you two headed?

NIGEL
Chicago.

MEGAN
That's where we live.

BECKY *(Glad to change the subject, she begins to remove her jacket)*
Really?

SAL
Get ready to hit some traffic.

MEGAN
The town's full of fruitcakes. They're stitching one of those giant quilts for AIDS...

MEGAN's POV: CLOSE-UP *of the looped red ribbon symbolizing support for AIDS patients on BECKY's lapel.*

...victims.

Long, awkward silence. MEGAN and BECKY stare at each other with curious disbelief.

NIGEL *(cheerfully)*
Well!
(Pause)
Who could possibly have imagined that a couple of Prairie View pom-pom girls would end up leading cheers from opposing political platforms, eh?

SAL
Yeah, how 'bout that?

Silence.

SAL *(rising)*
Excuse me, but we been on the road a long time, and I have to visit the john.

NIGEL *(hurriedly)*
Yes, I think I'll join you.

SAL
When you gotta go, you gotta go.

NIGEL
Quite right.

SAL
You two settle all the problems of the world while we're gone.

NIGEL
Yes, and take a crack at Northern Ireland while you're at it.

The women are not amused by their husbands' remarks.

SAL
Honey, order me steak and eggs with ketchup and a bottomless cup of coffee.

NIGEL
And Rebecca, dear, I'll have my eggs poached with either scones or brioche, orange marmalade, and Darjeeling tea, one lump.

The husbands head for the restroom.

SAL
Are you English?

NIGEL
Why, yes.

SAL
I myself of am Italian extraction.

NIGEL
Yes, I'd gathered that.

We catch Sal's expression as they disappear into the men's rest room.

BECKY
Sal seems very nice.

MEGAN
Thank you. Nigel seems very nice, too.
(Pause)
He calls you Rebecca?

BECKY
No one's called me Becky since high school.

MEGAN
Oh, I'm sorry. I can call you Rebecca, too.

BECKY
No, don't be silly.

After an awkward pause, they speak simultaneously.

BECKY & MEGAN
So how did you meet Sal/Nigel?

They laugh.

BECKY
Go ahead.

MEGAN
He fixed my drain.

BECKY
Sal's a plumber?

MEGAN
He was at the time. Now he has his own contracting business.

BECKY
Sounds like he's doing very well.

MEGAN
Yes. He put me through law school.

BECKY
Congratulations! That's terrific!

MEGAN
Thank you.

BECKY
What kind of law do you practice?

MEGAN
I'm deputy general counsel for Illinois Right To Life.

For a moment, words fail Becky. She nods pleasantly, then asks:

BECKY
Do you have any children?

MEGAN
Yes!

She reaches into her pocketbook for her wallet and displays some photos.

MEGAN
This is Joseph. He's four now. And this is Mary. She'll be two in August.

BECKY
They're lovely...hmmm...Joseph and Mary. How...traditional!

MEGAN *(not sure what to make of Becky's compliment)*
Thank you.

BECKY
Good spacing, too.

MEGAN smiles uneasily.

> MEGAN
> How about you? Do you and Nigel have any children?

BECKY pulls out her wallet and flips it open.

> BECKY
> We adopted Han-Jun from Korea in '97...

> MEGAN *(surprised)*
> Adopted? Why that's wonderful!

BECKY smiles uneasily, unsure of how she feels about Megan's approval.

> BECKY
> ...and this is little Chelsea. We adopted her from Romania.

> MEGAN
> They're both beautiful.

> BECKY
> Thank you.

> MEGAN
> So, where did you and Nigel meet?

> BECKY
> At a fundraiser for Hilary Clinton.

MEGAN looks down at her napkin, then up again.

> MEGAN
> Um...what do you do in Denver?

> BECKY
> Oh, where to begin. Nigel's with the National Labor Relations
> Board, and I'm a stay-at-home Mom.

MEGAN
Oh, I envy you!

BECKY
I serve on a few committees and do a lot of volunteer work…

MEGAN
That's terrific!

BECKY
…for Greenpeace and the AIDS Coalition.

MEGAN *(after a pause, and a little reluctantly)*
Did you know someone who had AIDS?

BECKY *(a little indignantly)*
Doesn't everybody?

MEGAN is silent.

BECKY
Are you serious? You haven't known anyone with AIDS or HIV?

MEGAN
You say it as if I should be ashamed of the fact.

BECKY
Well, I hope you're not proud of it!

MEGAN
I'm neither. Apparently we travel in different circles.

BECKY
Apparently so! I happened to know a few fruitcakes!

MEGAN
I'm sorry. I didn't mean to offend you.

BECKY takes a deep breath.

> BECKY
> I'm sorry, too.
> *(Pause)*
> Look, do you mind if I ask you a question?

> MEGAN
> No, of course not.

> BECKY
> How on earth did you get involved with those Operation Rescue people?

A big-haired WAITRESS approaches their table and overhears the next line.

> BECKY
> I can't believe that you could be taken in by a bunch of Bible-thumping clerics and bee-hived Tammy Wynette worshippers!

CLOSE-UP *of the waitress's name tag, which reads "Tammy."* PAN UP *slowly to catch her facial expression.* CUT TO REST ROOM.

> SAL
> So you're English, huh?

> NIGEL
> I am indeed.

> SAL
> You like Tom Jones?

> NIGEL
> I beg your pardon?

> SAL
> Tom Jones?

NIGEL
The novel?

SAL
No, the singer.

SAL mimics Tom Jones, singing in front of the bathroom mirror.

SAL
"It's not unusual to be loved by anyone, bah-dah-dah-dah-dah."

NIGEL
Oh yes, of course. The singer.

SAL
He's English, too, you know.

NIGEL
Welsh, actually.

SAL
You know, some girls used to say I looked like Tom Jones.

SAL unfastens a shirt button, and moves to imaginary music.

SAL
"What's new pussycat? Whoa-oa-oa-oa-uh!"

CUT TO BOOTH.

BECKY *(highly agitated)*
But you're murdering doctors!

MEGAN *(equally agitated)*
My God, Becky! How can you judge the entire pro-life movement by the actions of a lunatic fringe? Was the whole civil rights movement illegitimate just because the Black Panthers sold drugs and killed cops?

BECKY
I am really offended by that analogy!

MEGAN
Why? Because it rings true? Or because it doesn't serve your agenda?

BECKY
No—it's because you frame the issue so narrowly, and totally ignore the question of women's rights!

MEGAN
Sex selection abortions deny a woman's right to be born!

BECKY
How can you presume to know when life begins?

MEGAN
I don't. Do you?

BECKY
No! Of course not! But I'm not the one—

MEGAN
Fine. You don't know when life begins. I don't know when life begins. The Pope doesn't know. Faye Wattleton doesn't know.

BECKY
Then how can you presume to force your views on me?

MEGAN
How can you presume to destroy what may be a human life?

BECKY
Because it may not be.

MEGAN
Exactly. We don't know if we're committing murder. Therefore, we shouldn't gamble.

BECKY
What convoluted leap of logic leads you to that misguided conclusion?

MEGAN
Look: if there was a sheet hanging between us and the next booth, and I told you there might be someone sitting there behind the sheet, but there might not be, and then I handed you a gun and said it was perfectly legal to shoot, and you might be killing an innocent person but you might not be, because we really don't know if she is behind the sheet or not, would you pull the trigger?

BECKY *(slowly and deliberately)*
I choose to concentrate my compassion on human beings whom we know to be alive.

CUT TO GIFT SHOP, *where NIGEL is examining a porcelain figurine and SAL is leafing through an issue of* Easy Riders *magazine.*

SAL
You ride?

NIGEL
What's that?

SAL gestures to a photograph in the magazine.

NIGEL
Oh, no. I haven't ridden a motorbike in years.

SAL
You used to have a bike?

NIGEL
Yes, as a student at Cambridge. It was the only way to get around.

SAL
What kind of bike did you have?

NIGEL
As I recall, it was a B-S-A.

SAL
You had a B-S-A?

NIGEL
If memory serves.

SAL
I'd never buy a B-S-A.

NIGEL
Why not?

SAL
They're always breakin' down.

NIGEL
Oh. Well, what purchase would you recommend?

SAL *(taps a page in the magazine)*
Harley-Davidson. Chopped.

NIGEL
Chopped?

SAL
Chopped. I myself am the proud owner of a vintage, black & gold, customized 750 cc Harley Davidson chopper.

NIGEL
You don't say?

SAL
I do say.

NIGEL
Indeed? Do you ride it often?

SAL
Not lately.

NIGEL
Why not?

SAL
It broke down.

CUT TO BOOTH, *where BECKY and MEGAN are sitting in stony silence.* CUT BACK TO GIFT SHOP.

NIGEL
Say, old sport, do you ever work on old motorcars?

SAL
In Chicago, I am known as "master of the ganglia wrench."

NIGEL
A master craftsman! That's superb! You see I've got this positively ancient MG up on blocks in the gárage, and none of the Denver mechanics seem to be able to do a thing with it.

SAL
You got the right parts?

NIGEL
No, that's been rather a problem. *(beat)* I say, you wouldn't happen to know...

SAL *(raising a palm)*
Consider it done.

CUT TO BOOTH, *where BECKY and MEGAN have their noses buried in newspapers. NIGEL and SAL return in jovial humor.*

NIGEL
It's all settled then!

The women lower their newspapers.

NIGEL
Rebecca, dear, clear our calendar for Labor Day weekend with the Santangelos!

TIGHT SHOT *of the mortified women.*

FADE OUT.

Most Valuable Dictator!

Cast Of Characters

Game Show Emcee
Idi Amin
Fulgencio Battista
Francisco Franco
Benito Mussolini
Adolf Hitler
Female Model
Josef Stalin

Setting

A Hollywood Awards Ceremony

Time

The mid 1990s.

AT RISE:

Lights up brightly with music: a snappy arrangement of "Hooray For Hollywood." A tuxedoed and perfectly coiffed EMCEE bounds out to center stage. He hosts the show in a style that is equal parts Miss America contest, Academy Awards ceremony and Tournament of Roses parade.

EMCEE *(to audience)*
And now...the category you've all been waiting for! The nominees are...

HE opens a gilt-edged envelope, pulls out a gold-leaf card, and reads with great enthusiasm.

EMCEE
First—from the exotic jungle empire of Uganda, where trumpeting pachyderms play nightly anthems in his honor: President Idi Amin!

Applause track and theme music: "Colonel Hathi's March" from Disney's "The Jungle Book." AMIN ENTERS from left and promenades across the stage in full military regalia, waving magisterially to the crowd. He stops and stands in a designated spot, DOWNSTAGE RIGHT.

EMCEE
From sunny Spain, stomping ground of the legendary Don Quixote de la Mancha, and spiritual home of impossible dreamers everywhere, Generalissimo Francisco Franco!

Applause track and theme music: Overture from "Man of La Mancha." FRANCO ENTERS bedecked in his familiar Fascist uniform. HE mimes the knight errant on his steed, and crosses the stage where he joins AMIN. They greet each other warmly, then stand at attention.

EMCEE
From gay Havana, Cuba's carnival city and play land of the Caribbean, El Presidente, Fulgencio Battista!

Applause track and theme music: Tito Puente's "Rumba! Rumba! Rumba!" BATTISTA ENTERS in a white silk suit of the style he was known to wear at the gaming tables of 50s-era mob casinos in Havana. HE rumbas across the stage to AMIN and FRANCO, who form a conga line and dance behind BATTISTA.

EMCEE
Whoa! Hold on there, you party animals! There's more to come!

AMIN, FRANCO, and BATTISTA return to their places and stand sheepishly.

EMCEE
From Rome, the eternal city, in romantic Italy, the black baron of bombast, Il Duce, Benito Mussolini!

Applause track and theme music: a tarantella. MUSSOLINI ENTERS wearing his traditional black uniform with Shriner's cap and tassel, and dances a jig across stage where he joins the others. MUSSOLINI folds his arms, juts his chin high in the air and nods vigorously.

EMCEE
Our fifth and final nominee, from the beautiful Berghof, his verdant mountain villa overlooking enchanted Berchtesgaden: der Fuhrer, Adolf Hitler!

Thunderous applause interspersed with shouts of "Heil!" Martial music: Wagnerian Nazi anthem. HITLER ENTERS in brown storm trooper outfit, swastika armband, black boots and riding crop. As he walks across stage, HITLER acknowledges cheers with his characteristic, limp-wristed Fascist salute. The other four dictators embrace him.

EMCEE
And now…

EMCEE pulls a new envelope from his breast pocket and begins to open it suspensefully.

EMCEE
…the winner in the category of Most Valuable Dictator is…

EMCEE pulls out a gold-leaf card—pauses melodramatically—and reads:

…der Fuhrer, Adolf Hitler!

More thunderous applause. Reprise Wagnerian anthem. The other dictators embrace HITLER and kiss him on both cheeks. HITLER steps to the fore, weeping with gratitude. EMCEE hands HITLER a handkerchief and gestures to someone offstage. A beautiful female MODEL in swimsuit ENTERS, walks over to HITLER and places a stain sash over his shoulder. It falls diagonally across his chest and reads, "Most Valuable Dictator." HITLER tries to speak to the audience but is so choked by emotion that words fail him. The other dictators gather round him to lend moral support. The EMCEE stands aside, touched by the moment.

Suddenly and unexpectedly, JOSEF STALIN appears in the far left wings, dressed in a World War II vintage, olive brown uniform of the Red Army. HE crouches and beckons urgently to the EMCEE.

STALIN
Psssst!

The EMCEE is startled by the surprise appearance of Stalin. No one else seems to notice him. Lights dim on the other directors, who continue to congratulate Hitler. Crowd noise fades to an undercurrent.

STALIN
Psssst!

The EMCEE slowly and reluctantly approaches STALIN, who is visibly upset. THEY stand together in a pool of light, UPSTAGE LEFT. The EMCEE is clearly uncomfortable and embarrassed by this turn of events. Throughout the conversation that follows, HE continues to look over his shoulder, as if afraid that someone will spot Stalin.

EMCEE
Uh…hiya, Joe.

STALIN
Why wasn't I nominated!?

EMCEE
Now, take it easy, Joe.

STALIN
I was intentionally excluded!

EMCEE
Now, Joe, I don't have anything to do with the nominations.

STALIN
You're lying!

EMCEE
The academy makes the nominations, Joe. I just read 'em.

STALIN
I refuse to ignore this insult!

EMCEE
Now, Joe, easy does it.

STALIN
I demand recognition!

EMCEE
Now, Joe, don't take it personally.

STALIN
How can I not take it personally?!

STALIN stretches out an arm and points at HITLER. Lights up briefly on HITLER and the other dictators. HITLER is still basking in the glow of his victory.

STALIN
That…that…vagabond from Vienna is getting all the attention again!

EMCEE
Now, now, Joe, that's not the way it is, at all.

STALIN
He's always in the spotlight! It's never me!

EMCEE
It's just politics, Joe.

STALIN
Since the end of the war, his character has appeared in more than three hundred feature films! I'm only in one movie! Just one! And it was made-for-TV! Not even a theatrical release!

EMCEE
Now, Joe, there's a good reason for that.

STALIN *(throwing a tantrum)*
Why?! Why?! Give me one good reason why Hollywood glorifies his legacy and buries mine in the dustbin!

EMCEE
C'mon, Joe. You're a crafty old pol. Think about it.

The EMCEE gestures toward HITLER and the others. Lights up briefly on the five dictators.

EMCEE
Look at them. Don't you get it? They're all right-wing. They're an embarrassment to the other side. Especially Hitler. It serves our purpose to keep him visible. Any time we want to destroy a conservative, we smear him by raising the spectre of Hitler. Works like a charm, time and again: Goldwater, Nixon, Pat Buchanan, Robert Bork, Clarence Thomas, Newt Gingrich...You know the drill.

STALIN *(stomping his feet)*
But it's not fair! Even by the most moderate estimates, it's a fact that I am responsible for ordering the execution of twenty million innocent people—more than double the number that Hitler can claim!

EMCEE
Shhhhhhhh!

STALIN
And I don't get anywhere near the recognition he does!

EMCEE
No one is singling you out. Do you see another left-wing dictator here? Huh? Is Mao Tse Tung here? Is Fidel Castro here? Is Ho Chi Minh here? Has anyone made any movies about them?

STALIN
But—

EMCEE
Think about it, Joe: has Hollywood ever made a movie about a left-wing dictator?

STALIN fumes silently.

EMCEE
Of course not. We want to keep the focus on <u>them</u>.

HE gestures toward Hitler and the other dictators.

EMCEE
Look at that, will ya? It's a PR bonanza.

STALIN squirms, unable to counter the Emcee's argument.

EMCEE
It's political, Joe. It's not personal.

STALIN burns in silence.

EMCEE
Look, Joe, you gotta understand. This is not a good time for you to pop up.

EMCEE looks over his shoulder again, and speaks conspiratorially, in a whisper.

EMCEE
We finally have one of our people in The White House. And she got there by pretending to move to the middle. You're a former commander-in-chief. You know military strategy. It was a classic Trojan Horse gambit. Don't go blowing our cover.

STALIN
But my legacy is being lost forever!

EMCEE
Not forever, Joe. You'll get your due. Just be patient. But we can't have you parading around the country in high profile. The voters will catch on. Just lay low for a while. Give us a few more years to layer the federal government. By then, the bureaucracy will be so massive that it won't matter. Socialism will metastasize, and the very nature of daily life in this country will take on the quality of a visit to the Department of Motor Vehicles.

Pause.

There'll be no turning back.

Pause.

Then, you can come out of hibernation and Hollywood will make a few movies about you. Trust me, Joe. Your day will come.

STALIN is grumpy but resigned to his fate.

STALIN
It's not fair.

EMCEE
Look, Joe, I gotta get back out there. Now, please—go sit in the back somewhere or up in the balcony. And lay low, will ya?

Lights down on STALIN, who EXITS LEFT. The EMCEE moves UPSTAGE RIGHT and stands alongside HITLER in the spotlight. The other four dictators give Hitler one last pat on the back and EXIT RIGHT. The EMCEE begins to interview HITLER.

EMCEE
So, Adolf. I understand you're starring in a new romantic comedy?

HITLER
Yes. A remake of *"An Affair To Remember."* I co-star with Eva Braun. Mel Brooks will direct.

EMCEE
Sounds like a winner. Tell us about it.

HITLER
Well, as the movie opens, I'm in my underground bunker in Berlin with Eva. Then we flash back...

Fade Out with music: Frank Sinatra singing "I'll Be Seeing You, in all the old familiar places..."

END OF PLAY

Roberto Duran At The Harvard Business School

CAST OF CHARACTERS

Roberto Duran, a slum-spawned Panamanian boxer and 4-time world champion whose savage style made him a legend among fight fans. Mid-40s.

Executive MBA candidates from about a dozen companies. Three actors can play all of these corporate roles. At least one should be female. Early 30s.

A United Way campaign manager. Late 20s.

SETTING

A lecture hall at the Harvard Business School.

TIME

The mid-1990s.

AT RISE:

A heavy bag embroidered with the brand "EVERLAST" dangles from a chain above center stage.

A round bell rings. THREE MBA CANDIDATES, all lean executive sharks in pinstripes, ENTER carrying briefcases, and march to their desks.

Opposite a chubby fellow wearing glasses, a baggy sweatshirt, and earth shoes ENTERS carrying a knapsack and whistling *I'll Get By With A Little Help From My Friends*. HE waves and nods pleasantly to the other three. They don't acknowledge him. HE stops whistling and shrinks into a seat. All sit silently for an uncomfortably long moment.

Music: *The Lonely Bull*. ROBERTO DURAN appears before his class dressed in a hooded black robe and boxing trunks. He radiates a blisteringly bad-ass aura, and slams a taped fist into the heavy bag with startling violence.

DURAN

I define the word "professional" as one who does it for the money. That means there are certain similarities between your business and mine.

In the ring and in the market, we are at war. And in order to prevail, we must be intelligent warriors. Able to analyze problems and opportunities. Set clear objectives. Devise workable strategies. Execute tactics, and measure performance.

Case study number one: My title bout with Davey Moore. June 1983. The problem? He was a lot younger than me. The opportunity? To exploit his inexperience. The objective? To take away his middleweight title.

DURAN (cont.)

Now, what strategy would solve the problem, seize the opportunity, and meet the objective?

[A show of hands among his students.]

DURAN

Yes, the brand manager from IBM.

EXECUTIVE #1

To me it recalls the situation we faced in the early 80s when Apple was dominating retail sales of personal computers.

DURAN

And how did IBM respond to that challenge?

EXECUTIVE #1

We leveraged our access to superior market intelligence data to bypass retail outlets and sell direct to national accounts, and within two years garnered a 60 percent share. Apple never knew what hit them.

DURAN
(nods approvingly)

Very similar to the "blind" strategy I used in the Davey Moore fight. Midway through the second round, I thumbed him in the left eye. It swelled shut so he couldn't see the right hand coming. The result? A third-round T-K-O and two point five million dollars for nine minutes work.

[UNITED WAY raises his hand.]

DURAN

Yes, the campaign coordinator from United Way.

UNITED WAY

But doesn't such a tactic raise ethical issues?

[The other students eye him coldly. Long, stony silence.]

DURAN

I beg your pardon?

UNITED WAY

Um…ethics?

[Pause]

A sense of decency?

[Pause]

Knowing right from wrong?

[Long, uncomfortable pause]

DURAN

It is right to disable your opponent. It is wrong to be disabled by your opponent. That was covered in a prerequisite course.

[The other students snicker.]

UNITED WAY

Oh…

DURAN

Case study number two: My comeback bout against Iran Barkley. A legendary but aging fighter emerges from inactivity to reclaim the title from a younger competitor. Now, what does that bring to mind?

[A show of hands.]

DURAN

Yes, the product planner from Polaroid.

EXECUTIVE #2

Procter & Gamble reestablishes market supremacy for Crest with the new tartar-free formula?

DURAN

Good contemporary example. Others. Yes, the systems engineer from Motorola.

EXECUTIVE #3

Fuji buys sponsorship rights to the 1984 Olympiad but Kodak locks up all the network air time and actually gains share.

DURAN

A textbook example of ambush marketing, but more like the "knee to the groin" strategy I used in my first fight with Sugar Ray Leonard—a bout that's also instructive from the standpoint of psychological one-upsmanship between evenly matched rivals. Who recalls the key tactic there?

[A show of hands.]

DURAN

Yes, the investment banker from Morgan Stanley.

EXECUTIVE #1

Wasn't that the bout where you gave his wife the finger at ringside?

UNITED WAY

The finger?

EXECUTIVE #3

The finger.

DURAN

Correct. And what did that accomplish?

EXECUTIVE #2

It infuriated Leonard, disrupted his concentration and threw him off-stride—much as we did to the board of Kraft Foods while engineering their acquisition by Philip Morris.

DURAN

Philip Morris! [beat] A company that saw its core business come under ferocious assault by public interest groups and the federal government. Who sees the obvious parallel?

[A show of hands.]

DURAN

Yes, the lobbyist from Nestle.

EXECUTIVE #3

In the same way that the federal government is moving slowly to outlaw cigarette smoking, Congress periodically threatens to ban boxing.

DURAN

Precisely. In each case, we see the weight of regulatory agencies bearing down on the practice of free enterprise.

[EXECUTIVE #2 raises his hand.]

DURAN

Yes, the security analyst from Goldman-Sachs.

EXECUTIVE #2

In the case of Philip Morris, though, management had the foresight to hedge its bet and diversify successfully into dairy products and other retail food categories. I don't see that boxing has an equivalent option.

DURAN

Don't be so sure. [beat] But this student raises an interesting question. What must boxing do to survive a hostile regulatory climate?

[UNITED WAY raises his hand. DURAN reluctantly acknowledges him.]

DURAN

Yes…the gentleman from United Way.

UNITED WAY

Shouldn't boxing offer to step up efforts to police itself voluntarily?

DURAN

I'm afraid that volunteerism may have dulled your instincts for survival in the free market. Any other ideas? Yes, the account executive from Ogilvy & Mather.

EXECUTIVE #1

I think we're already seeing some receptiveness in the advertising community to accept boxing and help put a human face on the sport.

DURAN

In what way?

EXECUTIVE #1

Product endorsements that align the sport with leading brand names, which at least implicitly bestows respectability on the profession.

DURAN

I want examples. Yes, the creative director from Young & Rubicam.

EXECUTIVE #2

We sold Frito-Lay on the idea of using George Foreman in the Doritos spot.

DURAN

Good. Another. Yes, the media buyer from J. Walter Thompson.

EXECUTIVE #3

Right Guard gained three share points in minority markets where we ran a spot featuring Marvelous Marvin Hagler.

DURAN

And having fought Marvin, I found him quite credible portraying a consumer in need of a reliable deodorant product. [beat] Good, another example. Yes, the market research manager for Monsanto.

EXECUTIVE #1

I recall ads for Lee Myles Transmission as far back as the late 60s that featured Rocky Graziano.

EXECUTIVE #3

And the mid-70s spots with Muhammad Ali for Black Flag roach-killer.

DURAN

Each was a pioneering but risky tactic at the time because both fighters had had brushes with the law. Who can cite a more modern example of the risks involved with celebrity product endorsements?

EXECUTIVES #1 #2 AND #3 (in unison)

MIKE TYSON!

EXECUTIVE #1

We were all set to use him in a romantic spot for Paco Rabane cologne. That business with the beauty queen blew the whole deal.

EXECUTIVE #3

We had three reels shot and in the can with Tyson modeling Pierre Cardin evening wear. Had to junk the whole campaign.

EXECUTIVE #2

We were already airing his "safe sex" public service announcements in six markets. Do you know what pulling those spots cost me?

EXECUTIVE #3

Performance bonus?

EXECUTIVE #2

Out the window.

[Sadness and shaking of heads all around, except for UNITED WAY, who appears bewildered.]

DURAN

So we see the downside risk that any business takes by staking the reputation of its brand on a celebrity. In what other ways, though, might an enterprise such as boxing improve its image to help stave off regulatory constraints?

EXECUTIVE #1

I think boxing ought to take its cue from the example of youth soccer. I mean here's a sport that just a few years ago was a giant yawn in the domestic market. Now you'd be hard-pressed to find a middle-class suburb without a youth soccer league. Boxing ought to move in the same direction.

EXECUTIVE #2

Well, you've already got the Golden Gloves tournament.

EXECUTIVE #1 (shaking his head negatively)

Those are inner-city, minority dominated competitions that involve older teens. That's not the demographic profile I'm talking about. You've got to grab the youngest children of the most affluent parents.

[Throughout the exchange that follows, the EXECUTIVES gain rapid momentum and nod enthusiastically at each other's suggestions in a kind of mini-brainstorm.]

EXECUTIVE #3

You might start by establishing a boxing equivalent of the national youth soccer association.

EXECUTIVE #2

Follow it up with a direct mail campaign that targets the zip codes where we know per capita income exceeds $250K.

EXECUTIVE #1

We could bring in name fighters to make personal appearances at youth recreation centers.

EXECUTIVE #3

Or even designate a national spokesperson to serve as an ombudsman for boxing.

EXECUTIVE #2

Kind of like what Bill Cosby does for cigar smoking. You know, a benign and friendly face.

EXECUTIVE #1

We ought to get the sports editors of local newspapers behind the idea.

EXECUTIVE #3

Establish closer alliances with the mainstream sporting goods manufacturers.

EXECUTIVE #2

Nail down sponsorship agreements with Wilson and Spalding.

EXECUTIVE #1

It's a billion-dollar idea!

[UNITED WAY can stand this no longer. He bolts to his feet suddenly, and appears very agitated.]

UNITED WAY

Wait a minute! Doesn't the popularity of youth soccer depend on parents' desire for a safe alternative to football?

EXECUTIVE #3

So?

UNITED WAY

So how are you going to sell them on a sport that's even more dangerous to their children than football?

EXECUTIVE #1

That obstacle hasn't slowed the growth of classes in karate and the other martial arts.

EXECUTIVE #2

Besides, we can emphasize safety in the advertising and sales promotion for headgear.

EXECUTIVE #3

And in the wake of rising crime rates, I think we can really tap into a vein of fear among wealthy suburbanites.

EXECUTIVE #1

Parents will want their kids to have self-defense skills.

EXECUTIVE #2

Particularly as we experience the kind of urban sprawl that spreads gang warfare.

DURAN

I think you've hit on exactly the kind of bold initiative we seek to generate in these seminars, and what's more, you're showing the same kind of ring savvy that I relied on in my welterweight title bout with Pipino Cuevas. Who remembers what happened?

[A show of hands.]

DURAN

Yes, the quality control manager from Xerox.

EXECUTIVE #1

As I recall, Cuevas hit you with a left hook in the first round, but you covered up effectively and he wasn't able to capitalize.

DURAN

Why not?

[EXECUTIVE #2 raises his hand.]

DURAN

Yes, the chemical engineer from Kodak.

EXECUTIVE #2

Cuevas seemed to lack the presence of mind to seize the window of opportunity.

DURAN

Or, in the parlance on my profession, he lacked…

DURAN (cont.)

[DURAN cups a hand to his ear.]

Class?

EXECUTIVES #1, #2, AND #3 (in unison)

The killer instinct!

DURAN (nods affirmatively)

An abundance of which was displayed during the fourth round of the same fight.

EXECUTIVE #1

Early in that round, you rocked Cuevas with a right hand. But instead of proceeding tentatively as he had in the first round, you pounced on him and put him away. It was vicious. It was brutal. It was savage. It was like...

EXECUTIVE #2

Like Wal-Mart gobbling up a grocery store.

EXECUTIVE #3

Like Scott Paper through a state forest.

EXECUTIVE #1

Like Nintendo's massacre of Milton Bradley.

DURAN (humbly)

Thank you, all of you, for those very flattering analogies. The point, though, and I think you've grasped it very well, is that an opponent's weakness must be exploited swiftly...relentlessly...unmercifully.

[UNITED WAY raises his hand. DURAN acknowledges him, again quite reluctantly.]

DURAN

Yes—our friend from United Way.

UNITED WAY

I don't mean to keep sounding discordant notes here. I really don't. But aren't there ways that businesses can cooperate with one another? And work together for the broadest possible benefit to society?

[Boos, moans, and groans all around. DURAN holds up his hand to silence the class.]

DURAN

Now, now, there's no need for that.

[DURAN beckons United Way, summoning him to rise and come to the front of the classroom.]

DURAN

What's your name, son?

UNITED WAY

Theodore Benson.

DURAN

Where you from, Ted?

UNITED WAY

Berkeley, California.

DURAN

You went to school there?

UNITED WAY

Yes. I have an undergraduate degree in social work.

[Snickers from THE EXECUTIVES. DURAN holds up his hand again.]

DURAN

I'm going to level with you, Ted. And I don't want you to take this the wrong way. I mean, everybody's different. To each his own. [HE sighs.] But, I really don't think this is the right program for you. [Pause.] I could be wrong, but...well, I think you should know that beginning in about five minutes there will be a seminar on early childhood development in the education building next door. I can't help but think you might feel more at home in that class.

[Long silence.]

UNITED WAY

But…I don't want to study early childhood development.

[DURAN eyes UNITED WAY sharply for a long moment, then turns and walks to the desk of another student, where he grabs a sheet of loose-leaf paper, then begins tearing it into little pieces and littering the ground with them.]

DURAN

You see these little pieces of paper, Ted? Pretend that each represents a thousand shares of Microsoft, currently trading at ninety dollars per share on the New York Stock Exchange.

[DURAN finishes spreading the pieces around. There are perhaps two dozen little squares of paper on the floor. The EXECUTIVES lean forward in their seats with anticipation, and shuffle their feet anxiously, like racehorses at the starting gate.]

DURAN

Now, tell me Ted: how should we determine who among us wins a controlling interest in the company?

UNITED WAY

Divide the shares up equally so everyone gets a fair amount?

[The EXECUTIVES snicker.]

DURAN

No, Ted.

UNITED WAY

Have the government regulate the distribution according to need?

[More snickering.]

DURAN

No, Ted.

UNITED WAY

Set aside a proportional number of shares for women and minorities?

[More snickering.]

DURAN

No, Ted. I'm afraid you just don't get it.

[DURAN moves off to the side of what will become The Arena.]

DURAN

To your corners!

[The EXECUTIVES rise and move to three corners of the stage.]

DURAN

I want a clean fight!

[THE EXECUTIVES steel themselves for action.]

DURAN

No rabbit punches, head butts, or low blows, and remember to protect yourself at all times!

[Each EXECUTIVE assumes a boxer's crouch, fists cocked for fighting. After a suspenseful pause, DURAN rings a round bell. The EXECUTIVES spring out onto the floor, fighting each other for scraps of paper in a furious melee. UNITED WAY hesitates until DURAN extends an open palm inviting him to join the fight. UNITED WAY reluctantly wades into the battle. He reaches tentatively for a scrap of paper and immediately receives a punishing blow to the head. HE is batted about mercilessly for the duration of the fight, which lasts perhaps thirty seconds, ending when DURAN sounds the bell to conclude the round. The EXECUTIVES stop fighting and return to their seats. UNITED WAY wobbles unsteadily to his feet.]

DURAN
(pointing in sequence to each of the EXECUTIVES)

How many shares?

EXECUTIVE #1

Eight thousand!

EXECUTIVE #2

Eight thousand!

EXECUTIVE #3

Eight thousand!

[UNITED WAY's hands are empty, and he is too beaten and battered to respond.]

DURAN (to United Way)

You see, Ted, if you aim for excellence, you achieve fairness. If you aim for fairness, you achieve…nothing.

[UNITED WAY is beyond bewildered, appearing almost in a state of shock.]

DURAN
(points toward a door offstage)

Early childhood development.

[UNITED WAY staggers toward the wings and EXITS.]

DURAN
(shakes his head sadly)

It wasn't my intention to embarrass that young man, but rather to illustrate a point for you: he exemplifies a naturally occurring phenomenon that is most prevalent in personnel departments and, to a somewhat lesser degree, among public relations and package design people.

[Pause]

I call it "nice guy syndrome."

[Pause]

It is dangerous, and it is contagious. If you catch it, I assure you it will derail your career.

[A buzzer sounds. The EXECUTIVES begin to gather up their papers and pack their briefcases.]

DURAN

Okay, for next week, I'd like you to review the films of my fight against Carlos Palomino. I'll be discussing the subject of "Media Bias Against Big Business," and I want you to pay particular attention to the hostile questions posed to me at the post-fight press conference by Howard Cosell.

[Pause]

Until then…

[DURAN slams a first into the heavy bag.]

…keep on slugging!

[Lights out quickly.]

END OF PLAY

The Day The Dumpster Spoke

CAST

A single actor whose voice we hear but whose face we never see.

Half a dozen upscale party guests who are seen only in silhouette.

SETTING

A back alley behind a windowless brick building.

TIME

Election night, 1992.

AT RISE:

Stage right we see a large rectangular, cast-iron dumpster jutting out from the loading dock of the building's cargo bay. The top of the dumpster is sealed over and welded shut. Stage left, behind a screen representing a wall of the building, we see the silhouetted shapes of guests at a party. It is a black-tie affair. Aristocratic chatter about activist governance and public policy. A television anchorman announces election returns, and the news is greeted by cheers, the popping of corks, the fizzle of champagne, and the clinking of crystal. The party noise fades slowly. There is a long moment of silence. The dumpster speaks:

DUMPSTER

Oh, God. Oh, God. Why? Why couldn't I have been the hull of a ship? A cruise ship. A luxury liner. The love boat. Why couldn't I be carrying honeymooners to Honolulu? Sailing along in the South Pacific, my cabins booked to capacity with coppertoned couples who lay about my decks, listen to my lounge singer and then make love all night, letting the gentle rhythm of the waves do all the work. That would be so much better. So much better than this. Anything but this…but not this.

Pause. We hear more election returns. The party noises ebb and flow, then are drowned out as the DUMPSTER wretches, heaves, tries to vomit its contents—but cannot.

DUMPSTER

Oh, God. Oh, God. Please recycle me. It doesn't have to be something glamorous. I'd do just fine as a Sears-Kenmore top-loading washer-drier. I'd be serving a necessary function, meeting a basic need for some family. I'd even work in a laundromat. I'm not proud. I'd work anywhere. Anywhere but here. Anything but this.

Pause. We hear more election returns, followed by cheering from the party guests, who in turn are drowned out by the DUMPSTER, retching and heaving again, more violently than before.

DUMPSTER

Oh, God. This is horrible. This is worse than being an oven at Auschwitz. Why this? Why me? I'd rather be a sewer, or a toilet. A public toilet. A toilet in a subway. A toilet in a prison. Then at least I could flush away the secrets and the shame and the sorrow they've sealed inside me. Oh, God, blow me up, blow my top, explode me like a volcano, spew my guts across the country and let them land on every doorstep, let them stick to every windshield, let them smack against the windows of The White House. Let them see…let them see…Oh, God, let them see.

The DUMPSTER begins retching violently, shuddering visibly and shaking the entire set for an uncomfortably long moment. Then it stops. There is a brief silence, ended by the voice of the network anchorman projecting the winner of the presidential election. Party guests roar their approval, and break into an impromptu chorus of Happy Days Are Here Again. *We see the silhouettes of a man and a woman ascending a staircase to the roof, each gripping a champagne bottle. They open a trapdoor, tumble joyously onto the tarmac of the roof and begin making love behind the raised hatch. A shaft of light emerging from the stairwell illuminates the letters of an elevated sign. It looms over the front of the building but faces away from the alley so we view the rear of the letters and must read them backwards. They spell out:*

P-L-A-N-N-E-D P-A-R-E-N-T-H-O-O-D

The chorus of Happy Days Are Here Again *echoes and fades. Lights down on everything but the dumpster, which emits a final shudder.*

Fade to black.

END OF PLAY

If You Can't Say Anything Nice

CAST OF CHARACTERS

Paul, mid-20s
Cliff, a little older

SETTING

No place in particular.

TIME

No time in particular.

AT RISE:

PAUL is humming Stevie Wonder's "My Cheri Amour." There is an ease and freedom to his limbs that suggests he's floating on clouds of romance and happiness.

Then CLIFF enters.

CLIFF
What'd you do last night?

PAUL
Saw a great movie at the Metro! One of the best I've ever seen.

CLIFF
You liked that movie?

PAUL
Yeah. It was terrific.

CLIFF
I saw that movie. I thought it was terrible.

PAUL
Well, maybe it wasn't great. But it was good.

CLIFF
Oh, it was garbage!

PAUL
Well, it was pretty good.

CLIFF
Oh, it stunk!

PAUL
Yeah, I guess it was pretty bad.

CLIFF
It stunk!

PAUL
Yeah, you're right. It really stunk.

Long silence.

CLIFF
You go alone?

PAUL
Where?

CLIFF
To the movie.

PAUL
No, I took the girl who lives across the street.

CLIFF
The girl who lives across the street from you?

PAUL
Yeah, she's beautiful. Gorgeous. A knockout!

CLIFF
You think that girl's attractive?

PAUL
Yeah. She's really pretty.

CLIFF
No, she's not. She's homely.

PAUL
I think she's kind of pretty.

CLIFF
Oh, she's ugly!

PAUL
She's not so bad.

CLIFF
She's ugly as sin!

PAUL
Well, yeah, I guess she's pretty bad.

CLIFF
She's a dog!

PAUL
Yeah, I guess she is a dog.

Long silence.

CLIFF
You have a good time?

PAUL
Yeah. A great time!

CLIFF
You took a dog to a movie that stunk? And you had a great time?

PAUL
I think I did.

CLIFF
How could you have a great time with a dog at a movie that stunk?

PAUL
I don't know. Maybe it wasn't so great.

CLIFF
Maybe not.

PAUL
It seemed like I was having a good time, but maybe I didn't.

CLIFF
Maybe you imagined the whole thing.

PAUL
Maybe.

CLIFF
Maybe you didn't even go to the movie with that girl.

PAUL
Maybe not.

CLIFF
Maybe you only <u>wish</u> you went to a great movie with a beautiful girl.

PAUL
Yeah. You're right. I didn't really go.

Long silence.

CLIFF
Why do you paint red polish on your toenails?

PAUL
I don't paint red polish on my toenails.

CLIFF
Sure you do.

PAUL
No. Really. I don't.

CLIFF
Of course you do.

PAUL
I don't remember doing it.

CLIFF
I've seen you do it.

PAUL
You have?

CLIFF
Of course. Don't you remember?

PAUL
No.

CLIFF
Take off your shoes and socks.

PAUL complies. There is no red polish on his toenails.

CLIFF
See.

PAUL
I swear I don't remember painting them!

CLIFF
Well, there's the proof.

PAUL
I can't remember everything I do!

CLIFF
Okay, but don't lie to me.

PAUL
Okay.

Long silence. Paul puts his shoes and socks back on.

CLIFF
I've been elected to the United States Senate.

PAUL
You have?

CLIFF
Yes. By a landslide.

PAUL
I didn't even know you were running!

CLIFF
You should keep up with the news.

PAUL
But—the election isn't until next month.

CLIFF
They changed the date. They moved it up.

PAUL
They did?

CLIFF
Yes. Because I asked them to.

PAUL
They did that for you?

CLIFF
Yes. And I won. In a landslide victory of historic proportions. I am now a United States Senator.

PAUL
Wow. That's great.

CLIFF
Yes. I am a very powerful man now.

PAUL
I am lucky to have you as my friend.

Pause.

CLIFF
You're not my friend.

PAUL
I'm not?

CLIFF
No.

PAUL
I thought I was your friend.

CLIFF
How could I be friends with you? You don't keep up with the news.
You didn't even know I was elected senator. Am I right?

PAUL
Yes.

CLIFF
So, you didn't vote in the election, did you?

PAUL
No.

CLIFF
You say you're my friend, but I ran for the United States Senate,
and you didn't even vote for me. That's friendship?

PAUL
No, I guess not.

CLIFF
And what's more, you lie to me.

PAUL
I do?

CLIFF
Yes. You tell me you saw a great movie. But the movie stunk. Then you tell me you went to the movie with a beautiful girl. But she was a dog. Then I find out the truth is you didn't go anywhere with anyone. And then you denied you painted your toenails when in fact you had, as we both observed.

PAUL
I'm sorry.

CLIFF
Apologies aren't good enough. You're a pathological liar. A subversive. A danger to the state. And I, as a United States Senator, have a responsibility to the people of this country to put you behind bars.

PAUL
You're going to put me in prison?

CLIFF
Yes. I'm leaving now to summon federal security forces who will come here and arrest you.

PAUL
Do you have to?

CLIFF
Would you have me break my pledge to the voters of this country?

PAUL
No.

CLIFF
In fairness, I must inform you that the security forces of the state are notoriously brutal.

PAUL
They are?

CLIFF
Yes, they are. You would know that if you weren't so apathetic, and kept up with the news, and voted in elections.

PAUL
What will they do to me?

CLIFF
They'll beat you.

PAUL
They will?

CLIFF
Unless you do exactly as I say. Then they'll go easy on you.

PAUL
What do I have to do?

PAUL complies with each of CLIFF's orders.

CLIFF
Put your right arm behind your head and grab your chin.
Pause.
Now put your left arm behind your back.
Pause.
Now cross your left leg over your right.
Pause.
Now squat on your right leg.
Pause.
Now remain completely motionless until the security police arrive. If they find you this way, they'll go easy on you. Otherwise, they'll beat you.

PAUL
Okay.

CLIFF
And one other thing…

PAUL
What's that?

CLIFF
When they arrive you must be singing the new national anthem.

PAUL
There's a new national anthem?

CLIFF
Yes. A result of legislation I introduced in the Senate.

PAUL
What is it?

CLIFF
Peggy Lee's last hit song, from 1968.

PAUL
"Is That All There Is?"

CLIFF
You know it?

PAUL
Yes.

CLIFF
Good. It may save your life.

CLIFF exits. Still squatting, PAUL sings like Peggy Lee.

PAUL
"Is that all there is?
Is that all there is?
If that's all there is, my friend,
The let's keep dancing…
Let's break out the booze
And have ourselves a ball,
If that's all…there…is."

Silence. PAUL remains frozen for an uncomfortably long moment. We hear the opening verse of the Vienna Boys Choir singing Mozart's "Ave Verum." A white dove flutters down to Paul and circles celestially around his head, freeing him, and flies off.

CLIFF re-enters.

CLIFF
You still here?

PAUL
Yep.

CLIFF
The security police didn't come?

PAUL
They came.

CLIFF
Well?

PAUL
They weren't after me. They were after you.

CLIFF
After me?

PAUL
Yes.

CLIFF
That couldn't be.

PAUL
Oh, yes. They told me that you stuffed ballot boxes. That your election was a fraud. And that once elected, you abused your office. That you are guilty of malfeasance and misappropriation of funds.

CLIFF
No. I'm innocent.

PAUL
No. You're guilty. The security police had evidence.

CLIFF
They did?

PAUL
Yes. And that's not all. The chief of security is a first cousin of the girl I took to the movies.

CLIFF
But you didn't go to the movies.

PAUL
Yes, I did. The chief said so.

CLIFF
How does he know?

PAUL
He was at the movies.

CLIFF
The same night as you?

PAUL
He goes every night to see that movie.

CLIFF
Why does he do that?

PAUL
Because his brother directed it.

CLIFF
Oh.

PAUL
The chief of security is very angry that you said his cousin is a dog, and that his brother made a movie that stunk.

CLIFF
Oh, no!

PAUL
Oh, yes. What's more, I've been deputized.

PAUL hands CLIFF a bound scroll.

PAUL
This is a warrant for your arrest. My orders are to bring you in.

CLIFF
You wouldn't.

PAUL
I would.

CLIFF
Then all is lost.

PAUL
Not quite.

CLIFF
What do you mean?

PAUL
I have the authority to absolve you of your crimes.

CLIFF
Would you?

PAUL
If you will repent.

CLIFF
I will repent.

PAUL
Very well.

CLIFF
How shall I repent?

PAUL
Spread the gospel according to Thumper.

CLIFF
Thumper?

PAUL
That's correct.

CLIFF
From *"Bambi?"*

PAUL
That's correct.

CLIFF
What do you want me to do?

PAUL
Repeat after me: "If you can't say anything nice, don't say anything at all."

CLIFF
"If you can't say anything nice, don't say anything at all."

PAUL
Again.

CLIFF
"If you can't say anything nice, don't say anything at all."

PAUL
Again.

CLIFF
"If you can't say anything nice, don't say anything at all."

PAUL
Good. Now go and spread the word.

CLIFF
To whom?

PAUL
To anyone who may care to comment on this play.

BLACKOUT

Nativity Scene

CAST OF CHARACTERS

The Holy Family: Joseph, Mary, and the infant Jesus
A few Shepherds
Three Wise Men
A handful of Henchmen

SETTING

The stable in Bethlehem.

TIME

Then and now.

AT RISE:

Soft music: the first few bars of "The Little Drummer Boy." *A brilliant star rises over center stage, casting a beam of light down upon the stable of Christ's nativity.* **JOSEPH** *and* **MARY** *kneel on either side of the child Jesus, who is lying in his crib, surrounded by* **SHEPHERDS** *tending their sheep and cattle. The music fades. All is peace and tranquility.*

New music: the first few bars of "We Three Kings." *The* **THREE WISE MEN** *appear, stage left, and approach the stable. Reaching the crib, one of them addresses Joseph and Mary:*

WISE MAN

We come bearing gifts for the newborn king. Gold, frankincense, and myrrh.

The other two **WISE MEN** *present the gifts. Joseph and Mary nod appreciatively.*

WISE MAN

But we also come bearing sad tidings. King Herod, upon hearing of the birth of a new king, and fearing the emergence of a rival, has sent his legions out in search of the child, and has ordered them to kill all newborns.

Gasps of horror all around.

WISE MAN

You must flee, quickly, before—

Shouting is heard offstage:

VOICE (offstage)

There it is!

Suddenly the stable is overrun by officious men in contemporary dress who apprehend Joseph and Mary, hoist the child Jesus in his crib, and begin to haul them off. THE WISE MEN plead tearfully with the HENCHMEN:

WISE MAN

Please! I beg of you. Appeal to King Herod for mercy! Bade King Herod to spare the life of the child Jesus!

HENCHMAN (puzzled)

King Herod?

WISE MAN

Yes, your king. *(beat)* Are you not soldiers in the service of King Herod?

HENCHMAN

No...

Lights brighten to illuminate a backdrop revealing that the nativity stable has been erected to celebrate the Christmas season on the front lawn of a modern courthouse.

HENCHMAN

...we're on nativity patrol for the American Civil Liberties Union. *(To his co-workers)* Haul that thing off of government property!

HENCHMAN (cont.)

The child Jesus bolts upright in his crib and gapes pop-eyed as the ACLU men carry him off. Fade to black as music swells: an up-tempo version of "If I Had A Hammer."

END OF PLAY

The Three Ralphs

CAST OF CHARACTERS

Ralph Neas
Ralph Reed
Ralph Kramden
Moderator

SETTING

A network television news studio.

TIME

The mid-1990s.

AT RISE:

Talk show theme music. Four men are seated in directors' chairs. The MODERATOR sits at an angle so that he can face both the audience and his three panelists, who sit side-by-side facing the audience. The first two panelists wear business suits. The third wears a civil servant's uniform and carries a lunchbox.

MODERATOR
Good morning, and welcome to *"Newsmaker Sunday."* Our focus today: human rights. Our guests are: on the Left, the executive director of the Leadership Council on Civil Rights, Ralph Neas. On the Right, the executive director of The Christian Coalition, Ralph Reed. And in the middle, New York City bus driver Ralph Kramden.

Pause.

Gentlemen, the newswires report an escalation of violence over the weekend in Haiti. Things don't seem to be getting any better on the island. In hindsight, should we have sent the troops in? Ralph Neas, let's start with you.

RAPLH NEAS
President Clinton did the right thing and the compassionate thing. This was a clear case of a small bunch of rich landowners oppressing a poor black majority that had elected its own leadership. We took the right action by restoring President Aristide to power, and restoring democracy to Haiti.

MODERATOR
Ralph Reed, I sense you disagree.

RALPH REED
I do, indeed. The situation in Haiti posed no threat to the national interest of the United States. There was no compelling reason to put American lives at risk. It was an all too familiar example of do-gooding adventurism by a liberal Democratic administration.

MODERATOR
Ralph Kramden, your thoughts.

RALPH KRAMDEN
I agree with them.

MODERATOR
With whom?

RALPH KRAMDEN
With these guys.

MODERATOR
But they disagree.

RALPH KRAMDEN
They do?

MODERATOR
Yes.

RALPH KRAMDEN
Oh. Well, maybe they can talk it over and work things out.

MODERATOR
But what do you think, Mr. Kramden?

RALPH KRAMDEN
About what?

MODERATOR
About Haiti.

RALPH KRAMDEN
I oppose it.

MODERATOR
Oppose what?

RALPH KRAMDEN
Hating. I don't hate anybody. "Live and let live," I always say.

MODERATOR
No, Mr. Kramden. Haiti. Haiti. The island of Haiti.

RALPH KRAMDEN
I don't care where you live. On an island, in a desert, in a city. People should try to get along.

Pause.

MODERATOR
Yes. Well, let's get along to our next issue. In Northern Ireland, the Irish Republican Army truce is holding and President Clinton has pledged another $200 million in U.S. aid this year if the peace process moves forward. Ralph Neas, is this a wise expenditure?

RALPH NEAS
I think so. Anytime the United States can use its economic power to advance the cause of peace around the world, a greater good is served. Particularly when the promise of aid helps put an end to a vicious and centuries-old cycle of violence.

MODERATOR
Ralph Reed, you're hyperventilating.

RALPH REED
What about using that money to help offset the tax burdens on middle-class Americans? Northern Ireland is England's headache. England created the problem. Let England solve it. Northern Ireland is none of our business.

MODERATOR
Ralph Kramden, should the United States involve itself in Irish politics?

RALPH KRAMDEN
Well, speaking for the bus drivers, I think we should get Saint Patrick's Day off. *(beat)* I mean, the crowds along the parade route bring traffic to a standstill. You can't drive nowheres anyhow.

MODERATOR
Mr. Kramden, you mis—

RALPH REED
No, wait. If I may interrupt, Mr. Kramden has raised an issue that ought to be discussed here. And that is the foul behavior of parading Irish homosexuals who desecrated statues in St. Patrick's Cathedral!

RALPH NEAS
Oh, for God's sake…

RALPH REED
No, let's talk about this. I am perfectly willing to concede that the majority of homosexuals in this country are law-abiding citizens. But the vermin who defiled that cathedral ought to crawl back into their sewers!

RALPH KRAMDEN *(to Ralph Reed)*
Now wait a minute! I happen to know a very fine man who spends most of his life in the sewers.

MODERATOR
Gentlemen, please. Our focus this morning is on international relations. Let's move away from domestic social issues, and consider the administration's decision to extend most favored nation trade status to China. Ralph Neas, some are questioning whether the President is a vertebrate.

RALPH NEAS
Look, we have a better chance of improving the Chinese record on human rights by engaging them in trade and cultural exchanges than by isolating them. Cutting off dialogue with Dung Xiao Ping won't resurrect the dead of Tianenman Square.

MODERATOR
Ralph Kramden?

RALPH KRAMDEN
What?

MODERATOR
Your view of the Chinese record?

RALPH KRAMDEN
What record?

MODERATOR
On human rights! On how China treats its people!

RALPH KRAMDEN
Oh, I guess they treat their people okay. It's their dogs and cats gotta watch it. I mean, Alice won't eat at the Golden Dragon since they found those spare ribs came from a cocker spaniel.

MODERATOR
Mister Kramden—

RALPH NEAS
Excuse me, but Mr. Kramden has struck upon an issue of dire importance. Few causes in this world are purer of heart than the movement to safeguard animal rights.

RALPH REED
Oh, spare us!

RALPH NEAS *(to Ralph Kramden)*
I sit on the board of People For The Ethical Treatment of Animals.

RALPH REED *(to Ralph Neas)*
Spray-painted any fur coats lately?

RALPH NEAS *(to Ralph Kramden)*
Are you involved in any of the leading animals rights organizations, Mr. Kramden?

RALPH KRAMDEN
Yes, as a matter of fact. I'm proud to say I am a charter member of Brooklyn Lodge number 313 of the Royal Order of the Raccoon.

RALPH KRAMDEN removes his bus driver's hat and dons the coonskin cap of his lodge, waving the tail at Ralph Neas, who appears horrified.

MODERATOR
Mister Kramden, please. We're running out of time and I want to address the issue of Cuba. Should we re-establish diplomatic relations with Havana while Castro remains in power? Ralph Reed, let's start with you.

RALPH REED
Keeping the pressure on Castro is the only good thing Bill Clinton has done. Relenting now would be a disaster.

MODERATOR
Ralph Neas, is the president's "get tough" policy working?

RALPH NEAS
I think you're giving Bill Clinton more credit than he's due by suggesting that he even <u>has</u> a Cuba policy. For humanitarian reasons alone, we ought to help Castro feed and clothe the Cuban people.

MODERATOR
Ralph Kramden, we're almost out of time. You get the final word.

RALPH KRAMDEN *(to camera)*
Alice, you're the greatest!

MODERATOR
No, the final word about Castro! Castro!

RALPH KRAMDEN
Oh. Well, I don't know a lot about Castro's politics, but I'll say this for him: my back never felt better since I began sleeping on one of his convertible sofa beds. The man knows how to make a mattress.

MODERATOR *(after a sigh of exasperation, to camera)*
That's all for now. Join us next week on *"Newsmaker Sunday,"* when our panelists Ralph Neas, Ralph Reed, and Ralph Kramden will tackle the always sensitive subject of...busing.

Lights down as the theme from "The Honeymooners" *swells and fades.*

END OF PLAY

What're Friends For?

CAST OF CHARACTERS

MUTT
JEFF
SALLY

SETTING

A diner in Paterson, NJ.

TIME

The present.

FADE IN:

INT.   DINER   DAY

MUSIC: "Truck Stop Girl" by The Byrds. Two men approach the counter and take their seats. MUTT is short and stout. JEFF is tall and lean.

JEFF
Just tell her you love her.

MUTT
Just like that?

JEFF
Just like that.

MUTT
Just come right out with it?

JEFF
Just come right out with it.

MUTT
No lead up?

JEFF
No lead up.

MUTT
I don't know.

JEFF
What don't you know?

MUTT
It's too blunt.

JEFF
It's not blunt. It's honest. Women appreciate honesty in a man.

MUTT
Just blurt it right out?

JEFF
Blurt it right out.

MUTT
Here she comes.

JEFF
I'll give you some privacy.

SALLY, an attractive waitress, approaches to take their order. JEFF rises, walks to the jukebox, and pretends to read the selections.

SALLY *(with pot in hand, to Mutt)*
Coffee this morning?

MUTT *(leans forward across the counter, aggressively)*
I love you! I've always loved you! Ever since I first laid eyes on you! I must have you! I want you to be the mother of my children!

SALLY is startled. She gasps and drops the pot of coffee. It crashes to the floor and splatters, burning her ankles. She cries out in pain, grabs a towel, and hobbles away. JEFF returns to the counter and begins cleaning up the mess.

JEFF *(to Mutt)*
You're doing great.

MUTT
I made a fool of myself!

JEFF
Nonsense.

MUTT
She was scalded!

JEFF
She was overcome by emotion.

MUTT
I hurt her!

JEFF
You touched a place deep inside her.

MUTT
She hates me!

JEFF
She is captivated by the intensity of your passion.

SALLY returns. She eyes Mutt warily, then notices Jeff cleaning up the broken glass and spilled coffee.

SALLY *(to Jeff)*
Thank you.

JEFF
Don't mention it.

MUTT *(suddenly, to Sally)*
Are you captivated by the intensity of my passion?

SALLY *(aghast)*
What?!

JEFF
I'm sorry, Miss. Is this gentleman bothering you?

SALLY *(nervously)*
Yes…

JEFF
Would you like me to handle this?

MUTT
But you—you—

SALLY *(looks over her shoulder toward the kitchen)*
The manager's not here and I don't know what—

JEFF *(raises a palm)*
You go relax. I'll take care of it.

SALLY
Why, thank you.

MUTT
Oooooh, I could, I could—

JEFF
That's enough lip out of you, fella.

SALLY exits.

MUTT
What's the big idea?!

JEFF
It's all part of the setup.

MUTT
What setup?

JEFF
So you can show her.

MUTT
Show her what?

JEFF
That you don't let anyone move in on your girl.

MUTT
She's my girl?

JEFF
Of course she's your girl.

MUTT
I don't think she knows that.

JEFF
You're going to show her.

MUTT
I am?

JEFF
Yes.

MUTT
How am I going to show her?

JEFF
When she comes back here, I'll say to you: "Stop pestering this nice young lady or I'm gonna throw you out of here." Then <u>you</u> say, "Oh, yeah? She's my girl, buster!" and then throw a punch at me.

MUTT
Punch you?

JEFF
Knock me out.

MUTT
Knock you out?

JEFF
Cold.

MUTT
She'll be impressed?

JEFF
Of course she'll be impressed. She'll see that you don't let anyone move in on your girl.

MUTT
My girl?

JEFF
Your girl. We're gonna make it happen. Together.

MUTT
Gee, thanks.

JEFF
Don't mention it.

MUTT
I don't want to hurt you.

JEFF
Don't worry about it. I'll roll with the punch.

MUTT
This is really nice of you.

JEFF
What're friends for?

MUTT
I was beginning to wonder.

JEFF
Here she comes.

SALLY walks within earshot.

JEFF
Now, you stop pestering this nice young lady or I'm gonna throw you out of here!

MUTT
Oh, yeah? She's my girl, bust—

Before Mutt can get his punch off, JEFF knocks him cold with a short right hand.

JEFF *(to Sally)*
I'm sorry for all the trouble, Ma'am.

SALLY *(gaping at Mutt)*
What a nut!

JEFF
It must be very upsetting for you.

SALLY
What on earth could he have been thinking?

JEFF
Beats me.

SALLY
Well, thank you for helping.

JEFF
Are you okay?

SALLY
I could use a cigarette.

JEFF flips out a pack of Luckies. SALLY gestures to the "No Smoking" sign.

> JEFF
> Could you use some fresh air?
>
> SALLY
> I'm due for my break.
>
> JEFF
> There are some picnic tables nearby. We could have a smoke and...talk.
>
> SALLY *(gestures to MUTT, still out cold on the floor)*
> What about him?
>
> JEFF
> I'll call the highway patrol.
>
> SALLY
> I'll get my coat.

SALLY exits. JEFF grabs a glass of water off the counter and splashes it in MUTT's face, bringing him to.

> MUTT
> What happened?
>
> JEFF
> It worked.
>
> MUTT
> What worked?
>
> JEFF
> You won her sympathy.
>
> MUTT
> I did?

JEFF
She called me a cad for punching you out.

MUTT
She did?

JEFF
There were tears in her eyes.

MUTT
There were?

JEFF
She was bending down to kiss you when…when…

MUTT
When what?

JEFF
…when she realized she wasn't wearing any lipstick. So she went into the lady's room to make them rosy red for your first kiss.

MUTT
Our first kiss?

JEFF
She's going to awaken you with a kiss.

MUTT
But I'm already awake.

JEFF
Now don't go and spoil things for her.

MUTT
But—

JEFF
Close your eyes again.

MUTT
Close my eyes?

JEFF
And keep 'em closed or it'll ruin the moment.

MUTT
Oh, okay.

MUTT closes his eyes.

JEFF
But not here.

MUTT *(opening his eyes again)*
Not here?

JEFF
No. She insisted that I move you to a more comfortable spot.

MUTT
She did?

JEFF
Swore she'd call the cops on me unless I helped you.

MUTT
What a woman…

JEFF
C'mon. I told her I'd lay you down in a booth over there…

He points off-screen.

…with a few folded napkins for your pillow.

JEFF helps MUTT to his feet. They begin to exit toward the booths.

JEFF
Now, remember: keep your eyes closed. Don't open them, and don't move until you feel the touch of her lips against yours.

MUTT stops for a second and takes both of Jeff's hands in his.

MUTT *(near tears with gratitude)*
Thanks.

JEFF
You can thank me later. Now go lie down in that booth over there, and keep your eyes closed.

MUTT EXITS. SALLY ENTERS, and sees that MUTT is gone.

SALLY
Where'd he go?

JEFF *(helping her on with her coat)*
He came to when I was on the phone. Heard me talking to the highway patrol and took off like a bat out of hell.

SALLY
Go figure.

SALLY EXITS WITH JEFF. CUT TO MUTT, eyes closed, lying in the booth.

MUTT
What a pal…

FADE OUT

Under Glass

CAST OF CHARACTERS

Marge, a 50-ish executive secretary

SETTING

An executive suite

TIME

The late 1980s.

AT RISE:

MARGE stands outside the door of her boss's office, which slams suddenly and loudly in her face. Slowly, but with a firm sense of purpose, she opens the door again.

MARGE

But Ms. Hudson, I don't think anyone will <u>believe</u> that you've already left for the day. Besides, I just spoke to Marketing. Marketing says it's a Manufacturing problem. Manufacturing says it's a Quality Control problem. Quality Control says it's a Legal problem. And Legal says that when a camera crew from *"60 Minutes"* camps out in the lobby, it becomes <u>our</u> problem. There's simply no one else to turn to and—

Long pause.

If I may, Ms. Hudson, I must say that hiding under your desk and weeping isn't going to help. *[beat]* We've faced these situations before, and we'll face this one, too. Each of your predecessors had <u>his</u> baptism of fire. Did Mister Moore hide when John Stossel accused us of dumping mildewed infant formula in the Philippines? No. Did Mister Keller hide when Jesse Jackson announced to the world that we were selling surveillance equipment to South Africa? No. Did Mister Elliott hide when Ralph Nader wrote that our microprocessors were radioactive? No. *[beat]* You can't hide either, Ms. Hudson. You must find strength in the knowledge that no matter how severe it may seem today, a communications crisis always passes. By tomorrow, today's newspaper will be at the bottom of a birdcage, and CBS will be off chasing down some story about another nut tampering with Tylenol, another Exxon tanker leaking oil, or another synthetic breast leaking silicone.

MARGE (cont.)

[beat] We will be old news in no time. And in this case, remarkably, we may even be innocent. Mike Wallace will trot out ten of his scientists who'll swear that methylene chloride emissions are carcinogenic. We'll trot out ten of our scientists who'll swear that they're not. The whole story will bog down in boring arguments over parts per million, people's eyes will glaze over, and they'll go channel surfing. *[beat]* We <u>do</u> have to find that mother whose backyard borders the Elmgrove plant, the one with the smoking well water who keeps blaming us for her daughter's deformity. That's the kind of TV we don't need. But she'll keep quiet if we do what we did with that man who lived near the research laboratories, the one whose toilet kept backing up with white mice. *[beat]* Just buy her land at three times the market value, and offer to pay the girl's medical expenses if she'll sign a gag order. It's worked before, it'll work again. Now, I want you to come out from under your desk, sit right down at your computer...that's it, that's it...and write a short, concise statement denying—

A laptop comes flying out of the office and crashes at Marge's feet. Long pause. MARGE walks to her desk, picks up the phone, and hits a button.

MARGE

Reception, please. *[beat]* Pam? Marge. It may be another minute or two. Order them some coffee and Danish. Use the Corporate Communications charge number.

MARGE hangs up the phone and returns to the doorway.

MARGE

Ms. Hudson, I don't mind telling you that I was <u>not</u> among the women of this company who rejoiced over your appointment. Some of us had hoped that the position would go to a woman who'd risen through the ranks, a woman who had paid her dues, who'd accumulated a few battle scars along the way, who'd <u>earned</u> the right to manage communications for this company. *[beat]* To my dismay, the board decided that in this "age of electronic media," as they put it, the job called for a spokesperson who was more "telegenic," as they put it. My quarter-century with this company didn't help me in that regard, Ms. Hudson. And I will admit that it was particularly galling when the position went to a woman whose most salient credential to date was that of having once co-hosted the telecast of the Tournament of Roses Parade! *[beat]* Nevertheless, out of a sense of professionalism, and in the faint hope that you might open some doors for a future generation of women here, I put my personal feelings aside and resolved to serve you as loyally as I served your predecessors. But I will <u>not</u> sit idly by and watch while the first female vice president in the history of this company flutters in her Ferragamos when she comes face-to-face with her first crisis! *[beat]* Just what did you expect here, Ms. Hudson? That you were going to spend all your time smiling for photographers as you handed out checks to local charities? Well, I'm sorry, Ms. Hudson, but there is a pay-to-pressure ratio in this business. They don't hand you three hundred and fifty thousand dollars a year to smile sweetly for the cameras and give grants to community centers. They pay you <u>that</u> kind of money to go eyeball-to-eyeball with the likes of Morley Safer, and not to blink! *[beat]* Do you think you can just walk in here, accept your company car, your club memberships, your stock options, and all the other perks that your male predecessors have enjoyed, and not accept the angina, the ulcers, and the migraine headaches they had?

MARGE (cont.)

Why do you think men <u>die</u> before we do? When Mister Moore resigned, his breastbone looked like the map of a railway junction! Mister Keller was popping nitroglycerine when he keeled over in the washroom! And Mister Elliott took early retirement when the board decided that a stroke victim who drooled from the left side of his mouth wasn't "telegenic" enough! *[beat]* What did you think? What did you think?! That you'd won admission to some mahogany pan-eled men's club where old chums reminisce about school, slap each other on the back and do deals over drinks? No, Ms. Hudson! These are the tall grasses of the corporate Serengeti, and big cats are on the prowl! You're in the killing fields of the Fortune five hundred!

MARGE composes herself, takes a deep breath, and walks to her own computer terminal.

MARGE

Now, <u>I</u> am gong to sit down and compose a short, concise response to *"60 Minutes."* And <u>you</u> are going to deliver that response as calmly, as coolly, and as professionally as any male director of cor-porate communications would under similar circumstances.

MARGE sits and types.

MARGE

"Because...the...matter...in...question...is...being...litigated...
in...state...superior...court...and...the...magistrate...hearing...
the...case...has...advised...both...sides...to...refrain...from...
influencing...its...outcome...by...making...injudicious...
statements...to...the...media...we...will...abide...by the...
wishes...of...the...court...and...make...no...comment...
at...this...time."

MARGE prints the statement, rips it from the printer, rises, and walks to the door.

MARGE

Now take this, memorize it, and rehearse it until you sound as smooth as…as…as the queen of the fucking Rose Parade!

The trembling hand of a woman with long polished nails and a jeweled bracelet dangling from her wrist emerges from the doorway. The hand reaches tentatively to take hold of the printed statement. Slowly fade to black.

END OF PLAY

Free Fall

"Hello, Sid? This is Cy. She's fine. Forget her.
Shut up. A US Air jet just crashed near Pittsburgh.
Killed a hundred and thirty-two people.
Yeah. Fifth US Air crash in five years.
Yeah, yeah, horrible, horrible, tragic, tragic.
Shut up. Where'd US Air open this morning?
No! The New York Stock Exchange, you idiot!
I pay you not to know these things? C'mon.
Fifty-five? And where is it now? C'mon, c'mon.
Fifty…forty-nine…forty-eight…forty-seven.
Weeee got a freeee faaalll!
Weeee got a freeee faaalll!
I say the bottom is around thirty.
Shut up, Sid. When she hits twenty-nine, you
Gobble up every goddam share you can get your hands on.
Shut up. Call me. G'bye. And Sid.
…Do the same thing with Boeing."

The Straight Man

I'm the one who sets the stage
And often earns a smaller wage
Than he who gets the laughs.
I'm the one who throws the pies
And suffers when a punch line dies
And takes the blame for any gaffes.

My name is second on the bill
And believe me it's a bitter pill
To swallow come the curtain.
For after the applause and cheers
It's not for me they buy the beers
But for my partner, that's for certain.

I lob my lines across home plate
So crowds will think my partner's great
And never know he's selfish.
Sometimes I'd like to strangle him,
Torture him and mangle him,
Then poison him with day-old shellfish.

I'm Ollie, I'm Abbott, I'm Larry
I'm not the guy girls marry
Or even give a second glance.
For in the grander scheme of things,
God doesn't give the straight man wings,
Just another pair of baggy pants.

Saint Joseph Sunday Missal

Imprimatur † Francis Cardinal Spellman,
Blessed the book of future nuns and genuflecting bellmen.
His stamp upon those gold-leaved pages
Authenticated liturgy and prayer of prior ages
Or so thought children of parishioners
Who'd made the Church's mission theirs.

Plaid-clad legions filled the pews, reciting ancient creeds,
As black-and-white Dominicans thumbed their rosary beads,
Inhaling sacramental theatre with incense from a thurible
Too inebriate to doubt that Lazarus was curable
Or that stillborn souls are suspended for eternity.
In Nomine Patris, et Filli, et Spiritus Sancti.

And yet there are residuals
In memories of rituals.
The scent of God rising from a votive candle
How purple vestments favored Father Randle,
In the morning light of St. Augustine's sacristy
Introibo ad altare Dei.

"Fold your hands," said Sister Miriam
To lines of loyal cherubim
Who marched the Stations of the Cross
Never knowing what a loss
Of faith we'd feel in years to come.
Per omnia saecula saeculorum.

What cause had altar boys to doubt the testaments
When God anointed Catholic presidents?
And Bishop Sheen on Friday nights,
Whose ratings floored the Gillette fights.
"Life Is Worth Living" was the name of his show.
But in middle age, we wonder: Et cum spiritu tuo?

And at the varnished altar rail, all on bended knee,
With tongues outstretched, girls winked at me.
I held a gold communion plate underneath their chins
Assented to the absolution of their sins,
And ached with secret urges to see more than their faces
Pater Noster, qui es in coelis?

That's the memory I treasure most:
Watching them receive the Host.
For reflected in that golden plate, along with once familiar faces
I see the years when I believed that God would deal me aces.
Years that were better, years that were best.
Go now, the Mass is ended. Ite, misa est.

0-595-31918-1

Printed in the United States
20957LVS00001B/256-405

9 780595 319183